S0-BKT-920

With best wishes,

Gerald A Michaelson

Building Bridges
to Customers

Management Master Series

William F. Christopher
Editor in Chief

Set 3: Customer Focus

Karl Albrecht
Delivering Customer Value: It's Everyone's Job

Robert King
Designing Products and Services That Customers Want

Wayne A. Little
Shared Expectations: Sustaining Customer Relationships

Gerald A. Michaelson
Building Bridges to Customers

Eberhard E. Scheuing
Creating Customers for Life

Ron Zemke
Service Recovery: Fixing Broken Customers

Building Bridges to Customers

Gerald A. Michaelson

PRODUCTIVITY PRESS
Portland, Oregon

Management Master Series
William F. Christopher, Editor in Chief
Copyright © 1995 by Gerald A. Michaelson

All rights reserved. No part of this book may be reproduced or utilized in any form or by any means, electronic or mechanical, including photo-copying, recording, or by any information storage and retrieval system, without permission in writing from the publisher. Additional copies of this book are available from the publisher. Address all inquiries to:

Productivity Press
P.O. Box 13390
Portland, OR 97213-0390
United States of America
Telephone: 503-235-0600
Telefax: 503-235-0909
E-mail: staff@ppress.com

Book design by William Stanton
Cover illustration by Paul Zwolak
Graphics and composition by Rohani Design, Edmonds, Washington
Printed and bound by Data Reproductions Corporation in the United
    States of America

Library of Congress Cataloging-in-Publication Data

Michaelson, Gerald A.
    Building bridges to customers / Gerald A. Michaelson.
        p. cm. -- (Management master series)
    Includes bibliographical references and index.
    ISBN 1-56327-147-8 (hardcover)
    ISBN 1-56327-094-3 (paperback)
    1. Consumer relations. 2. Customer services. 3 Consumer satis-
faction. I. Title. II. Series.
HF5415.5.M53   1995
658.8' 12--dc20   95-12448
                                                        CIP

00 99 98 97 96 95 10 9 8 7 6 5 4 3 2 1

— CONTENTS —

PUBLISHER'S MESSAGE

The *Management Master Series* was designed to discover and disseminate to you the world's best concepts, principles, and current practices in excellent management. We present this information in a concise and easy-to-use format to provide you with the tools and techniques you need to stay abreast of this rapidly accelerating world of ideas.

World class competitiveness requires managers today to be thoroughly informed about how and what other internationally successful managers are doing. What works? What doesn't? and Why?

Management is often considered a "neglected art." It is not possible to know how to manage before you are made a manager. But once you become a manager you are expected to know how to manage and to do it well, right from the start.

One result of this neglect in management training has been managers who rely on control rather than creativity. Certainly, managers in this century have shown a distinct neglect of workers as creative human beings. The idea that employees are an organization's most valuable asset is still very new. How managers can inspire and direct the creativity and intelligence of everyone involved in the work of an organization has only begun to emerge.

Perhaps if we consider management as a "science" the task of learning how to manage well will be easier. A scientist begins with an hypothesis and then runs experiments to observe whether the hypothesis is correct. Scientists depend on detailed notes about the experiment—the timing, the ingredients, the amounts—and carefully record all results as they test new hypotheses. Certain things come to be known by this method; for instance, that water always consists of one part oxygen and two parts hydrogen.

We as managers must learn from our experience and from the experience of others. The scientific approach provides a model for learning. Science begins with vision and desired outcomes, and achieves its purpose through observation, experiment, and analysis of precisely recorded results. And then what is newly discovered is shared so that each person's research will build on the work of others.

Our organizations, however, rarely provide the time for learning or experimentation. As a manager, you need information from those who have already experimented and learned and recorded their results. You need it in brief, clear, and detailed form so that you can apply it immediately.

It is our purpose to help you confront the difficult task of managing in these turbulent times. As the shape of leadership changes, the *Management Master Series* will continue to bring you the best learning available to support your own increasing artistry in the evolving science of management.

We at Productivity Press are grateful to William F. Christopher and our staff of editors who have searched out those masters with the knowledge, experience, and ability to write concisely and completely on excellence in management practice. We wish also to thank the individual volume authors; Diane Asay, project manager; Julie Zinkus, manuscript editor; Karen Jones, managing editor; Lisa Hoberg and Mary Junewick, editorial support; Bill Stanton, design and production management; Susan Swanson, production coordination; Rohani Design, graphics, page design, and composition.

Norman Bodek
Publisher

INTRODUCTION

To achieve outstanding customer service, numerous components must be coalesced into a delivery system.

Each senior manager interviewed for this book was asked, "What are the key ingredients for achieving service quality?" Implied in that question is the understanding that senior leadership has the responsibility for designing the structures and systems necessary for implementing and sustaining an outstanding service delivery system. The ultimate effectivenesss of that system on the front line differentiates the great from the good.

At seminars on service quality, I often ask participants to name their most favorite and least favorite airlines. The same brand names are always mentioned as preferred. When I ask what makes the difference between the best and worst airlines, the most frequent response is "the way you are treated by people."

However, the people in the best and worst airlines come from the same national labor pool. It's not that one airline hires friendly, helpful people and the other hires unfriendly, unhelpful people. Rather, the difference is in the management systems that empower people to deliver service.

Having the right system is only the first step. All services are delivered by people. The best systems fail when people fail. This book is about the interaction of people within systems focused on serving the customer.

Bridges to customers are structured with a combination of systems and relationships. No matter how good the structure, people will not cross over regularly without a reason. The service relationship is a vital ingredient in the reason why customers keep coming back.

Good relationships are bred by bad systems and structures, just as bad relationships are bred by bad systems and structures.

1

BASIC ENGINEERING

When the early Romans built a bridge, the engineer who designed the structure stood under the arch as the scaffolding was removed. This clearly established his personal responsibility for good design. Many of these bridges are still standing today.

The responsibility for designing bridges to customers belongs to each individual and his or her team. The only people we can call customers are those who regularly cross over our bridges to us—or want us to cross over to them.

MEET THE ENEMY

Each of us is the architect and builder of the bridge of our own success or failure.

In a cartoon strip episode, Pogo and Albert are playing war. Pogo puts his field glasses to his eyes, looks down the road, and brilliantly exclaims, "Albert, Albert, we have met the enemy and they is us!"

I clearly recall the corporate meeting where after receiving input about failures in a product's performance, a senior executive sagely commented, "It is true, the enemy *is* us!"

It is true, the people most often standing in the way of our own success are us. I know people who have read a book that changed their lives. But when other people have read the same book, nothing happens. It's a paradox that an idea works well for some people and not at all for others.

There are no easy rules that can make us more successful in our mastery of how we build bridges to win customers. People become our customers only when they believe we can provide what they want. What works for one individual may not work for another. However, no system works unless we do.

It's not easy to acknowledge that we may be the enemies of our own success. It's too easy to blame others. Too often we look into mirrors distorted by our own egos. Instead of seeing the truth as others see it, we see only the truth we want to see.

To understand ourselves, we must learn how to glean the truth from the words we hear. It's much easier to be wise about others than it is to be wise about ourselves. The bridges in this book are based on lessons I learned from wise people who "know that they know."

Types of People
from Whom We Can Learn

The person who doesn't know, and doesn't know that he doesn't know:

He is a fool, shun him.

The person who doesn't know, and knows that he doesn't know:

He is a student, teach him.

The person who knows, and doesn't know he knows:

He is asleep, awaken him.

The person who knows, and knows that he knows:

He is wise, follow him.

—Anonymous

KNOW YOUR CUSTOMER

We build bridges to our customers by knowing where they are and what they want.

At a corporate meeting, the major topic of conversation was why the new dog food wasn't selling. Well-meaning participants offered a variety of logical reasons ranging from poor packaging to inadequate advertising. A new trainee who had recently visited the homes of several purchasers meekly offered the real reason: "The dog food isn't selling because the dogs don't like it!" If the dogs don't like it, it's not dog food!

The more time we spend internally talking about what the customer wants, the more likely we are to make the wrong decisions about what the customer wants. People become our customers only when they believe we can provide what they want.

To learn what the customer wants, nothing is better than talking personally to the customer. Even then we make mistakes because our minds filter the data so we see only what we want to see, or we transform a few suggestive observations into "fact."

The most successful products and services are developed by people who spend a lot of time studying the customer. The *Wall Street Journal* has identified Wegman's in New York State as the Harrod's and Nordstrom of groceries. Here you'll find store managers holding Saturday morning focus groups with 8 to 10 customers, or visiting a customer's home with a bag of groceries to find out why they haven't been to the store recently. These are just a few of the customer-oriented reasons why Wegman's store volume is four times greater than the average grocery retailer.

If we had been fishing in the Southwest a few years ago, a truck might have stopped and the occupants would have offered to clean and lubricate our fishing reels. They would have asked questions about what we liked and disliked about our fishing equipment. That information was then used to design a superior, competitive product.

The collection of knowledge occurs at several levels:

- Who are our customers?

- What do they want?

- How can we best provide what they want?

Our ability to collect information, listen objectively, and perform at the height of our professional ability depends on the accuracy of the answers to these questions.

Get to Know Our Customers Better

- **Ask questions.** Get customers to talk. What they have to say is more important than what we have to say.

- **Be curious.** Ask more questions.

- **Do research.** Find out everything we can about our customers.

- **Observe.** What's the significance of anything the customer is wearing. If at their place, look at the surroundings. If at our place, look at the accessories they've brought along.

A REGULAR CUSTOMER IS PRICELESS

The best bridges encourage customers to make a lifetime of repeat purchases.

When John Self arrived at his favorite rental car counter at the Wilmington, Delaware, airport, he asked how things were going. The agents told him that although they'd been very busy and were out of cars, they saved one for him since he was a regular customer. Self expressed his appreciation and went to pick up his assigned auto. When he opened the door, however, he stopped short because the interior reeked of dead fish. When Self returned to the counter to report the problem, the agents responded, "Yes, we know. We thought that since you were a regular customer you wouldn't mind." Outraged, he replied, "You've got it backward. The reason you don't want to give me *that* car is because I *am* a regular customer." He immediately found a new supplier for his rental car needs.

The regular customer is a priceless treasure and should be treated like one: handled with care and guarded carefully from the damages of competition. Regular customers can be the most profitable customers. Because they trust their supplier, they unusually spend more money per visit and are more likely to purchase deluxe products.

Results of an auto industry study confirm the real value of regular customers:

- When customers were very satisfied, 57 out of every 100 returned to the same dealer.
- When customers were very dissatisfied, 8 out of every 100 returned to the same dealer.
- Very satisfied customers were seven times more likely to come back to the same dealer and make a purchase than very dissatisfied customers.

No wonder dealers with a high volume of satisfied customers need to spend much less for advertising—customer referrals work in their favor.

Other studies of customer satisfaction show that while very happy customers mention their satisfactory experiences to an average of 5 people, very unhappy customers spread the word about their unsatisfactory experience to 10 to 15 others.

These surveys firmly establish that very happy customers are profitable and produce referrals that generate more profit, while very unhappy customers work even more actively to generate a bad reputation. Since customers are more likely to talk about *very unsatisfactory* experiences than they are about *very satisfactory* experiences, it takes a lot of the very good to compensate for the very bad—or even the moderately bad.

Don't ever think about the amount of money the customer spends on a single visit. Instead, think about the lifetime value of the customer. For example, a typical automobile owner spends more than $100,000 for automobiles over his or her lifetime. And, the driver who spends only $10 a week for gas, will spend $20,000 to $30,000 for gas over a lifetime. The lifetime value of a grocery customer has been estimated at $70,000.

We should calculate the lifetime value of a customer and build bridges to get our fair share of that business. Then we should plan to encourage our customers to give us more than our fair share of that business.

Why Regular Customers Are the Most Valuable

- They spend more on each visit.

- They cost less to do business with.

- They understand our business and we understand theirs.

- They make repeat purchases, which accumulate to a lifetime value.

THE CUSTOMER IS ALWAYS RIGHT

The customer is always right simply because he or she is the customer.

At the entrance to Stew Leonard's in Norwalk, Connecticut—"The World's Largest Dairy Store"—the following words are chiseled into a very large rock:

- Rule Number One: The customer is always right.

- Rule Number Two: If the customer is ever wrong, reread Rule Number One.

These rules are an absolute—even when we think we are right and the customer is wrong. If we show the customer that he or she is wrong, we will probably lose that customer.

When I called a supplier concerning a problem, they acknowledged that others had also misunderstood their advertising, but refused to make any adjustment. As a result, I no longer choose to be a customer of that company.

When we lose customers it's not easy to get them back. Several years ago one of my associates showed me a mailing for a special offer that he received from Eastern Airlines. Shaking his head, he said, "They had their chance to make me a customer and they messed it up with poor service and lack of concern for my needs. For them to send me this offer is a waste of their money." Eastern went out of business a few years later.

At a store that sells shirts and ties, management diligently followed every complaint. When an adjustment was due, they gave a refund. When management determined not to make an adjustment, they patiently and thoroughly explained why not. When Robert Kahn became a manager of the store, he answered every complaint by writing the customer a letter of apology, making an adjustment or exchange as requested, and enclosing a free tie. He began to hear about people telling their friends that his store was a nice place to do business. And they told others, who told others, who told others.

BE THE VERY BEST

The bridges to being the very best are constantly being reengineered and improved. We must run fast to stay good, and even faster to get ahead.

"Every morning in Africa a lion awakens. He knows that he must run faster than the gazelle or he will starve. Every morning in Africa a gazelle awakens. He knows that he must run faster than the lion or he will die. It matters not whether we are lions or gazelles. Every morning we awaken, we must run."

—Anonymous

Everything on earth either gets better or it gets worse. It either grows or decays. As long as we are green and learning, we are growing. It's when we think we have all the answers that we are ripe and rotting. We must get better to stay good, and get even better to be the best.

- The customer wants the best from us—and deserves no less.
- The customer wants to be the best—and we can contribute to that goal.
- When our customer is the best—so are we.

For us to be the best requires mastery of our profession. To be a professional requires a lifetime of learning.

A professional is a person who must understand and apply scientific knowledge. Unless he does so, he will be buffeted by forces beyond his control. Given knowledge, the professional can choose courses of action. He remains in charge of himself and his work.

—*Harry Levinson*

Experience is a great teacher. However, other people's experience is the *best* teacher.

Rules for Getting Better

- **Seek information.** Those who are the best constantly seek information from others. One friend who is at the top of his profession subscribes to sixty publications. Another listens to tapes of conferences while driving in his car. These successful professionals are organized to receive a flow of information.

- **Get a guru.** This is a wise friend not directly involved in our business who can serve as an advisor. Since the guru is not involved, we can tell him or her anything without fear of harming our career. We have found a guru when we find someone whose wisdom stands the test of time.

- **Find a coach.** This is someone directly involved in our business. He or she might be someone at a higher level in our own company who will act as a mentor and sponsor.

- **Get lucky.** The harder we work, the luckier we get.

HAVE A WRITTEN PLAN

The best plans build the best bridges, and the best plans are in writing—always.

I have six honest serving men.
They taught me all I knew.
Their names were What and When and Where,
and Why and How and Who.

—Rudyard Kipling

When we can provide answers to those six honest serving men, we have a plan:

- *What* is our objective?
- *When* is the action planned?
- *Where* will the action take place?
- *Why* should we do it?
- *How* will it happen?
- *Who* will be involved?

The plan must be in writing. On a visit to Oklahoma City, I called a retail dealer I had known years ago while working for another company. I was referred to his home number. When I reached him, we agreed to meet for lunch. He told me that his business had failed and he had sold the store. Then he said, "I often think about the number of times you told me that I should have my business plan in writing. I never did. I often wonder if I would still be in business if I had a written plan."

If our plan is not in writing, it is not a plan at all. It may be a dream, or a vision, but most often a plan that is not in writing turns into a nightmare.

The Six Honest Serving Men

The easiest way to remember these "serving men" is to memorize Kipling's poem. When using the questions to write a plan, begin by asking:

Why are we taking this action (reason)?
What do we want to achieve (objective)?

How do we get to the objective (strategy)?

Then, follow *When, Where,* and *Who* in whatever order makes sense.

CONCENTRATE RESOURCES

Great bridges are built one at a time by people concentrated on the task.

When Peter the Great arrived at the Russian town of Dorport, he found that his generals had spent weeks firing their cannons against the towns strongest bastions with little effect. He issued orders to concentrate the fire on the weakest walls and within a week those walls were breached and the town surrendered.

Time and time again, history has proven that the army, the organization, or the individual with the strongest resources wins. They win even faster when they concentrate their strength against competitive weakness.

To win the heart and mind of the customer, we must focus resources. For example, McDonald's focuses primarily on the young fast-food customer; Domino's concentrates on home delivery of pizza; and The Olive Garden focuses on serving Italian food to families.

The importance of concentration was established by a famous military writer, Carl von Clausewitz:

> *Where absolute superiority is not attainable, you must produce a relative one at the decisive point by making skillful use of what you have.*

Where the product or service meets the customer is indeed the decisive point. In the competitive world, customers pay our price only if they clearly perceive a relative superiority in our product or service. We achieve this relative superiority only by concentrating resources on an objective. When we try to please everyone, we end up pleasing no one—and we have no relative superiority in our product or service.

The decision concerning how many resources to concentrate is a function of what it takes to win the customer and what the competitor is doing. Have you noticed how often several very good restaurants can be found in the same geographic area? The high performance of one requires others to achieve a high level of performance in order to compete.

To win, it takes the best available resources concentrated on delivering a relatively superior product and service to the customer.

Fundamental Issues in Building Bridges to Customers

- Use available resources.

- Produce a relative superiority.

- Deliver it to a decisive point.

2

BLUEPRINTS FOR GREAT BRIDGES

Some bridges are built to reach the customer. Other bridges are designed to make it easy for the customer to cross over to us. All great bridges provide for two-way traffic. The more diligently we extend our reach to the customer, the more frequently the customer is on our side.

UNDERSTAND YOUR PROCESSES

The first step in managing processes is to recognize the activities that comprise them. To learn more about processes, chart the flow of their activities.

"Welcome to the Omni Mandalay, Mr. Michaelson," I heard the doorman say shortly after he retrieved my luggage from the taxi. He escorted me to the reception desk, asking whether I had previously visited this hotel. At the reception counter, he introduced me by name to a receptionist, who cheerfully said, "Welcome back, Mr. Michaelson," as she entered my name into the computer.

How did the doorman know my name? How did the receptionist know I had been at the hotel before? It's all part of an orchestrated set of activities called a process—the way the work is done.

Here's how the doorman's greeting process is organized:

1. Move swiftly to get the luggage and read the guest's name on the luggage tag.

2. Address the guest by name and welcome him or her to the hotel.

3. Engage the guest in conversation and personally escort him or her to the front desk. Ask questions to determine whether this is the first or repeat visit. Get all of the information we can.

4. Link the guest to the front desk staff by introducing the guest by name.

   • If this is a repeat visit, signal the front-desk clerk by touching your earlobe during the introduction. (This signal enables the receptionist to determine whether or not to say, "Welcome back.")

   • Pass along any additional information about the guest after the introduction. (For example, "Mr. Michaelson is attending the travel writers conference," or "Mr. Michaelson just arrived by plane from Knoxville." This helps the front-desk clerk establish a dialogue to make the guest feel at home.)

Whatever steps the front-door attendant uses to welcome guests, we can chart their flow to show the activities in the arrival. The desk clerk now takes over with the registration process and links to the person whose process is escorting the guest and luggage to the room.

All work is a process. All frontline processes are direct bridges to customers. For example, restaurants have a variety of frontline processes: the customer-greeting process, the seating process, the order-taking process, the

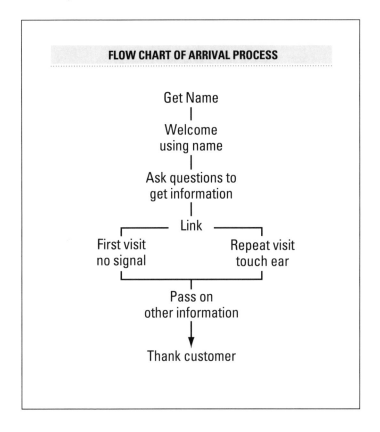

FLOW CHART OF ARRIVAL PROCESS

Get Name
|
Welcome
using name
|
Ask questions to
get information
|
Link

First visit   Repeat visit
no signal   touch ear

Pass on
other information

Thank customer

food-preparation process, the serving process—the list goes on. Processes that support the front line in a restaurant include cooking, purchasing, and accounting.

The first step in understanding the process is to assemble the people who perform the process and chart the flow of their activities on paper as a series of steps. It is amazing to see the differences of opinion and questions raised by people who supposedly do the same work the same way every day. The result is an understanding of the way the process is performed and where it begins and ends.

MAINTAIN HIGH STANDARDS

Process standards (and measurements against these standards) provide the mechanism to ensure that we build a sturdy bridge to the customer.

As you enter any Wal-Mart store, a greeter stands ready to advise you where to find what you are looking for. Ask directions to any area in fine hotels like the Halekulani in Hawaii, and you will be personally escorted to that area.

Every roll or croissant served at Au Bon Pain, the French bakery chain, must be fresh from the oven within four hours. Any bakery product over four hours old is given to charity.

Wal-Mart's greeter, Halekulani's escort, and Au Bon Pain's four-hour freshness are conditions for the performance of the process. These performance conditions are called standards. Too often, customer service processes have very few, if any, clearly defined standards.

In contrast, every manufacturing organization sets very specific standards for the products it makes: requirements must be met, dimensions must be exact, and tolerances must be attained. In every process, we find three basic types of standards:

- *Input standards:* ingredients that go into the process
- *Operating standards:* process activities
- *Output standards:* the results of the process

For example, in the food preparation process, input standards determine the quality and quantity of the ingredients. Operating standards determine the method of preparation—for example, how long to cook the food and at what temperature. And, output standards are concerned with the serving temperature, taste, and appearance of the food.

Input and operating standards have a significant effect on the quality of the output. Too often we try to improve the process simply by attempting to change the output (the results). It is always better to search upstream in the process in order to improve the process.

Aim for high standards. The higher the aim, the greater the stretch required to meet the standards, and the more likely it is that the output will please the customer.

All the processes must have standards, and everyone working in the process must know the standards. Standards provide a means of establishing process performance expectations and keeping managers from playing favorites. We must continually check all process standards against customers' requirements and expectations. Only when standards are established and clearly communicated can we measure and critique process performance. The measures of the process provide information that can ensure consistency of performance to the standards.

Using Standards and Measures

- Aim for high standards.
- Check the standards against the customers' expectations.
- Measure against the standards.
- Use input from measures to upgrade standards and improve performance.
- Look upstream for the most meaningful improvement opportunities.

GET BENCHMARKING INPUT

It is right to learn, even from the enemy.

—Ovid

At the Imperial Hotel in Tokyo, Managing Director Kiyohito Minoshima told me, "I visit my competitor regularly because I must know what he is doing. When I visit these hotels, I check in at the front desk and register for a room, stay overnight, and eat in their restaurants. On one trip to hotels in the United States, I took my staff along. Every evening we met to discuss what we had learned that day."

We can learn a great deal by looking at the delivery of products and services in our industry from the customer's point of view. Our customers acquire new levels of expectation every day as they do business with our competitors. The complete knowledge of what our customers are doing is only one more step in staying on the leading edge.

Too often, our competitive evaluation is confined to a comparison of prices or product features. Comparison becomes a methodology for improvement only when it studies comparable processes as processes. This approach is most often referred to as *benchmarking*. The goal of benchmarking is to find the best tools and methodologies for process performance and steal them shamelessly.

Basic Benchmarking

1. Select a process for comparison.
2. Organize a team of people who work in the process.
3. Thoroughly understand the process as a process.

4. Make a list of all of the places where we can learn more about this process.

5. Collect and evaluate this information.

6. Determine who does this process best. Look inside and outside our industry.

7. Screen this list to determine the benchmarking partners who provide the best information.

8. Develop a list of questions to ask.

9. Have a team of two or three people visit the benchmarking partners to ask the questions and observe their process in action.

10. Evaluate the data from all visits.

11. Incorporate the best into our process.

ORGANIZE THE POWER OF TEAMWORK

Build great bridges by strengthening the skills of individuals through the power of teams.

The following scenario is often established for participants at a Tennessee Associates International workshop:

"One of your people comes to you and says, 'The customer wants to know how many times the letter "f" appears in the following. Can you please give me the correct answer?' "

Note to reader: Try it! Count the number of times you see the letter "f" in the box on the following page. This is not a trick question. Do not look at page 25 until you have the right answer.

"f" Exercise

The necessity of training farm hands for first class farms in the fatherly handling of farm livestock is foremost in the minds of farm owners. Since the forefathers of the farm owners trained the farm hands for first class farms in the fatherly handling of farm livestock, the farm owners feel they should carry on with the family tradition of training farm hands of first class farms in the fatherly handling of farm livestock because they believe it is the basis of good fundamental farm management.

Count the total number of "f"s in this exercise ____.

Participants offer a wide range of answers that range from the low 20s to the mid-30s. As the answers are recorded, the audience chuckles because it seems ridiculous that such a simple question could have so many different answers. And yet, when they completed the exercise, most participants were fairly certain they had the absolute correct answer.

The participants then discuss methods for using the wide range of responses to determine the correct answer. One way is to consider their responses as votes, in which case, the correct answer would be the number with the most votes. Participants laugh at the absurdity of selecting the right answer in this ridiculous manner. Equally absurd is to declare the average of these numbers as the correct answer. However, we can all recall times when we used one of these methods to determine answers.

Participants then work in small teams of three or four to determine the correct answer. Usually, someone on each team suggests that each person count the number of "f"s on specific lines. They have discovered a process for getting the answer. Most often, every group now gets the right answer—proving that we get better results when we work together as a team than when we try to solve problems as individuals. And because they've determined a team process for getting the correct answer, they could also get the correct answer on any similar test. (The correct answer is 39.)

We have been conditioned to work as individuals, not as team members. That's why workshop participants first attempt to solve the problem as individuals and do not spontaneously work as a team or even discuss their answers with each other.

To build the best bridges to customers, we must learn how to work as members of a team.

Almost one hundred years ago, a French strategist stated the value of teams:

> *Four brave men who do not know each other well will not dare attack a lion. Four less brave who know each other well, and are sure of reliability and mutual trust, will attack resolutely.*

> *—Ardant du Picq*

Du Picq's statement illustrates the essence of teamwork in a nutshell. Teams are made up of people who know each other well. To operate effectively as a team, members must know how to use each other's strengths and weaknesses. It takes time to build the strong interaction and mutual trust of a high-performance team.

Ideas for Better Team Meetings

Before the meeting date:
- Advise starting and ending times.
- Circulate an agenda to all participants.
- Ask for additions or changes to the agenda.

At the beginning of the meeting:
- Set times for each item on the agenda.
- Appoint a timekeeper and a recorder.
- Establish operating rules.

At the close of the meeting:
- Make sure assignments are clear.
- Set the time and agenda for the next meeting.

IMPROVE AND INNOVATE

No bridge is ever as good as it can be.

At one time, when an F-15 crew chief in the U.S. Air Force ordered a needed part from the base warehouse it took hours for delivery. Moving the part through the system required 243 entries on 13 forms and involved 22 people and 16 employee-hours. Today, the crew chief walks a few yards to a computer to check inventory and makes a simple entry to advise parts storage to set the part aside. Then it's a short walk to a nearby warehouse where the part is or will shortly be waiting on the counter. Elapsed time is less than 10 minutes. These improvements were the work of General Bill Creech, head of the Tactical Air Command, and other members of his watch. Creech says, "Performance improvements are achieved by individuals, by collections of twos, and fives, and twenties, not by collections of a thousand or one hundred thousand. And, that's true in all organizations, not just the military."

We must continuously improve bridges that cross over to customers. The people who own the process are the best source of ideas for improvement.

Examples of worthwhile process improvements can be found everywhere. At the King Fahd Hospital in Saudi Arabia, it took only a few team meetings to determine how to reduce the billing process from 24 steps to 4 steps. At an ice-cream wafer factory in Michigan, a team checking temperatures throughout the length of a continuous-baking oven determined that variations in the temperature caused the wafers to curl into useless shapes.

I've checked into hotels where I've waited in long lines to register at the front desk and others where I've never waited in line. At a deluxe hotel, I completed the registration paperwork in my room; at a mid-priced motel I completed the registration from my car, just like I do at the drive-in counter at my bank. Both represent improvements in the usual registration process.

It's important to look at both macroprocesses (systems) and microprocesses for possibilities for improvement and innovation. The complete redesign of a process or system is often called reengineering. Whatever we do and whatever we call it, we must understand the process before we can improve it.

EXTEND A WARM WELCOME

The first step in getting the customer to cross the bridge is to offer a warm welcome—which is much more than just a friendly greeting.

The sound of a Chinese gong greeted me as I stepped from the airport limousine on arrival at the Grand Hyatt Bali. Then I realized for whom the gong sounded—it was indeed to welcome me. I bowed my head as a flower lei was placed around my neck. I knew then that I was really going to like this hotel.

When I arrived at The Conference Board reception lobby in their New York headquarters, I was greeted with a friendly "good morning" and a warm smile. The receptionist indicated a closet where I could hang my coat, offered me a newspaper, and asked that I be seated while she called the person I was to meet. I felt like this must be a great organization.

One hot summer day, as I boarded the courtesy van for the Atlanta Airport Hilton, the driver offered me a complimentary cold soft drink. When I arrived at the hotel, I was greeted with a friendly salutation by the doorman and every associate I encountered en route to the front desk. I marveled at the courtesy and thought this was a very good hotel.

What I found at each of these places was a warm welcome—the first step in building the bridge. I've also felt a warm welcome when I've called some organizations on the phone. The way some people say, "I'd be happy to ...," or "Certainly, Mr. Michaelson," lets me know that they feel good about providing a service.

Key Ingredients
of a Warm Welcome

- **No waiting.** Prompt service should follow immediate recognition. The longer the customer has to wait, the less warm our welcome seems.

- **Sincere friendliness.** Facial expression, tone of voice, and mannerisms distinguish warmth from efficiency.

- **A personal touch.** Greeting by name helps. If you can't, use the name as soon as you know it and link the customer to others.

- **Be helpful.** Determine what the customer needs and offer help. Don't be like cab drivers who offer a cheery hello and then watch while passengers load their luggage into the trunk.

- **Give accurate information.** Giving the customer wrong information can destroy good initial impressions. Send the customer to the wrong department, tell him or her the wrong times, or give bad information and that person will probably decide that the warm welcome wasn't warm at all.

UNLEASH THE POWER OF THE CUSTOMER'S NAME

The customer's name is an important component of any bridge. Use it again, and again, and again.

Know the customer's name. I've never found it easy to remember names, but I've always found it important to do so. When I worked for a company that took hundreds of customers on award trips to foreign countries, I spent weeks memorizing names and business affiliations.

As a result, when I read the customer's name tag, I could immediately respond with the name of their business and city. The personal recognition made them feel important and the appreciative expression on their faces was worth the effort.

When I was arranging my carry-on luggage aboard Singapore Airlines, a neighboring passenger casually commented: "Isn't this a great airline!" I can't recall what service triggered that compliment, but then it isn't any one thing that earns Singapore Airlines its high reputation. It's a lot of little things. The flight attendants frequently address me by name when I fly in business class on Singapore Airlines. Contrast the personal touch of Singapore with another airline, where the flight attendant addressed me only as 12B (my seat number) when I reminded her that I had ordered a special meal. Customers want recognition by name, not by number.

Use the name. During the Korean War, I visited a prisoner-of-war camp in South Korea. South Koreans, skilled in the art of getting information, were questioning a dozen North Korean prisoners seated in small cubicles. My guide explained that the cubicles were open so the prisoners could see each other talking to the interrogators.

Getting prisoners engaged in conversation was the first step. Next, it was important to use their names often in the interview. Interviewers found that if they addressed the prisoner by name five times in the first five minutes, they usually had a successful interview.

In those unusual circumstances, I first learned the awesome power of repetition of the customer's name.

Make a habit of using names. The best way to make someone a friend is to use his or her name frequently to indicate that we recognize him or her as an individual. This is a habit that must be learned.

In every service encounter, frequent use of the customer's name gives strength to the structure of that important bridge of a personal relationship. Think about it. Being addressed by name generates and reinforces a wealth of good feelings, such as:

- They are interested in me personally.
- They are giving me special attention.
- They know who I am.

Take pictures (when appropriate). As the lead person responsible for an annual conference of hundreds of customers, I arranged for a photographer to take pictures of people—making sure to include their name tags in the photo. Before the next year's conference, I studied the photos so I could more easily recall their names. Ever since, I've used the same basic technique in a variety of situations.

Use the Power of the Customer's Name

- Know the name.
- Repeat the name.
- Use the name regularly.
- Find ways to help recall it for the next encounter.

LINK THE CUSTOMER

Establish a bridge of links by introducing the customer by name to associates, and then strengthen those links by relating information about the customer.

"Yes," said the maître d' at Nicholas Nickolas restaurant, high atop the skyline of Honolulu, "I can have a table for two in a few minutes. Would you like to have a seat here or wait in the bar?" When I opted for the bar, he took my name, wrote it down, and said, "Thank you, Mr. Michaelson, please come with me." At the bar, he addressed the bartender, "Joe, Mr. Michaelson and his guest are waiting for a table and would like a cocktail." Joe responded, "Welcome, Mr. Michaelson, what would you like to order?" "Aha," I thought, "*the link system,*" as I recognized that the maître d' had verbally *linked* me to the bartender.

In Part 1, I used an example of the link system to illustrate the idea of processes—the way work is done. I first learned about the link system from Ronald Jones, O.B.E. (Order of British Empire), director and general manager of Claridge's in London. Now, halfway around the world in Honolulu, I had seen it in action. Jones told me he encouraged his people to use the link system; that is, to link each guest by name to another member of the staff just as one might introduce a friend to another friend. The link system is a neat way to link our relationship with a customer to another person in our organization.

Customer linkage should be a planned process in every organization. I've seen many circumstances where personal information was passed along with the introduction. This made friendly conversation easier for all. The additional background information often brought to the surface a commonality that helped form a bond of friendship.

Benefits of the Link System

- The link system requires:
    - ➤ knowledge of the customer's name
    - ➤ use of the customer's name
- Using the customer's name:
    - ➤ helps reinforce memory
    - ➤ impresses the customer
- Linkage by name helps the next person in the organization render service on a more personal basis.
- Use of the name by a number of people in an organization makes the customer feel like he or she is a guest among friends who know him or her as an individual.

GO TO THE LIMITS OF YOUR AUTHORITY

It is often better to beg forgiveness than to ask permission for an action. We can empower ourselves by assuming that we have all the authority we need except for that which is expressly forbidden.

At a restaurant in the San Diego Marriott Resort and Marina, I ordered a martini on the rocks and politely mentioned that I had been waiting for service. The waiter returned promptly with my martini in a glass without ice. "No problem," I said, "just bring me a glass with ice." He returned shortly to deliver a second martini on the rocks. "What's going on here?" I asked. "It's the drink you ordered, as ordered," he replied. I said, "But, now I've got two." He nodded in the affirmative. I asked, "Two drinks for the price of one?" He responded, "You weren't being taken care of properly; you deserve a free drink." When I inquired further, my friendly waiter explained, "When I see a problem, I'm *empowered* to take care of it. Management won't hassle me, even if I caused the problem." Ever since, I've been a friend of the waiter and that hotel.

This idea of empowerment also works in the successful Israeli Army, where field commanders operate under the principle that they have *all of the authority needed to do their job except that which is expressly forbidden.* Their success has been achieved by people who felt free to take action. They know that when people are waiting for permission, nothing is happening.

The losers in the race to win customers spend their time trying to find out what is expressly forbidden. Winners are testing the limits of their authority to serve the customer. At one very successful retail organization only two things are forbidden: chewing gum and stealing. Anything else is okay as long as it serves the customer.

On an assignment, I met separately with eighteen different field offices in the same company. The meetings started with participants giving input on the problems they were facing. In each of the eighteen offices, I observed the same pattern: The discussion evolved from figuring out how they could get management to solve the problem to determining how they, themselves, must solve it.

The derelict leaning against the lamppost watching successful people pass by was heard to mumble, "There but for me go I." That says it all. Our actions determine our success. Too often, the reason we don't build a bridge to the customer is because we don't test the limits of our authority.

MAKE IT EASY TO DO BUSINESS WITH YOUR ORGANIZATION

Customers return to bridges they find easy to cross.

High-performance organizations follow a few simple rules to make it easy for their customers to access their services.

Answer the phone promptly. The time interval between telephone rings is five seconds. At many successful organizations, the standard is to answer incoming calls on or before the third ring—that is, within 15 seconds. While waiting for the phone to be answered, I count the number of rings, and I often find that I've waited a minute or longer.

Some organizations play music while callers wait for an operator; others have organized systems to make sure phones are answered promptly. There's no question which is better.

Return calls promptly. When I called a charity concerning a donation, I received a call back a week later from a manager who explained he had been on a business trip to a nearby city. That poor excuse soured me on that organization. There's never a good excuse for not returning calls promptly.

The best organizations use the sundown rule. They return all customer calls before the sun goes down, even if it is simply to call and advise that further information will be provided the next day.

Keep waiting time to a minimum. Although I do not like waiting, I don't mind waiting to get into restaurants where the food is great. That's the reason they are crowded.

At a receiving dock in the United States, they serve lemonade if the incoming line of trucks gets too long. At a receiving dock in Asia they have figured out how to schedule incoming trucks so there is no waiting.

Some organizations provide refreshments to customers who have to wait in line. I prefer doing business with those who have figured out how to eliminate lines.

Organizations that have a bridge of easy access understand that if the customer has to wait too long, he or she will reconsider whether they want to be a customer.

Having a product or service that has a high level of demand is one thing; having customers wait is another.

LISTEN, LISTEN, LISTEN AND AGREE, AGREE, AGREE

Great bridge builders bite their tongues, keep quiet, and listen to what the customer has to say. Then they ask questions to get more information so they can solve the customer's problem.

A retail dealer complained to the manufacturer's agent, "I'm having problems with the stereo systems." The manufacturer's agent honestly admitted the existence of problems saying, "Yes, we are experiencing a high failure rate with the tape decks." To which the dealer replied, "What problems with the tape decks? My problems are with the amplifiers. You mean you're having problems with the tape decks, too?" Once again the problem of talking before listening was clearly demonstrated.

Socrates explained that the master of the dialogue is the person who is listening—not the one who is talking. He advised us to ask questions to gather information, then use that information to make our point.

Why do we think the way to get through to someone is to do all the talking? We can't get anything into someone's head unless we first listen to what is in his or her head. Listening serves two important purposes:

1. It helps others clear their thoughts so they can then listen to what we have to say.

2. It helps us discover how to make our idea more appealing to them.

And, while we are listening to customers, we should agree, agree, agree. Whatever the customer says, agree or remain silent, but don't argue.

We can learn alot about why not to start an argument from the Hatfields and the McCoys. Their feud lasted for many years. The longer they argued, the more each side was convinced they were right and the other side was wrong. The longer any argument continues, the more deeply each side becomes entrenched in their position, and the more difficult it is to get them out of that position.

I recall the time I started to criticize my advertising agency manager about the agency's last campaign. At the first opportunity, he interjected, "Jerry, you are absolutely right." I complained no more because with those few words of agreement he deflated my argument. How can we argue with someone who agrees with us? The discussion quickly moved on to the more positive aspects of how to correct the problem.

The bridge to winning is built on a foundation of two fundamental rules: listen, listen, listen and agree, agree, agree.

Keeping Communication Open

- Whatever we do, we do not argue with the customer.

- If the customer says, "Your company stinks," continue to listen intently, or say, "I understand how you feel."

- If the customer says, "Your product stinks," continue to listen intently, or say, "Please tell me more about your experience."

- If the customer says, "You stink," continue to listen intently, or say, "Thank you for being so honest."

- Don't say, "I agree, but..." The word but signals that you are going to present a rebuttal.

ANTICIPATE

Anticipate what customers want by looking at what they want from their own point of view.

While waiting for my luggage to appear at the baggage carousel in my hometown of Knoxville, Tennessee, someone from the airline paged me and asked me to come to the baggage office. The Delta flight attendant said that my bags had missed the transfer at the hub airport and would be on the next plane. He said that I should describe my luggage and go home. They would see that it was delivered promptly on arrival. Wow! That was better service than having it arrive on the same plane. Not only did I not have to wait at the baggage carousel, someone from the airline would send it home.

Contrast that with the situation I noted a few weeks later at a different airline at the same airport. While I was waiting at the ticket counter, a passenger arrived and interjected that his luggage was missing. The agent immediately answered, "You must be Mr. Mills. We have a wire that your bags missed the transfer and will be on the next plane." Since that airline had information concerning the missing bags, why couldn't they have paged him, saving him the time and aggravation of waiting until the last bag came off the carousel? Although the eventual service is the same (the bags are delivered at home), the difference between the way the two customers were treated makes a big difference in the way service is viewed. The perception of the way service is rendered is the most important reality.

At any Ritz-Carlton hotel, a customer's request for special service, such as a nonallergenic pillow, is entered into the computer. When that customer arrives at *any* Ritz Carlton anywhere in the world, the hotel provides a similar service.

Quality service doesn't happen *after* the customer complains; quality service is there when the customer arrives. Customers needs are anticipated and a bridge is built to meet their needs.

EXCEED EXPECTATIONS

Build a bridge of loyalty by giving more than a full measure.

At a silver mine in the hills of Colorado, I asked an old prospector to sell me a dollar's worth of silver dust. On one side of a balance scale, he placed a silver dollar. On the other side, he began to pour silver dust. When both sides were equally balanced, I knew I had a dollar's worth of silver dust.

But he didn't stop there. He kept pouring silver dust on my side of the scale until the scales were tipped way over in my favor. That was when I knew I had a real value because I received more than I expected. We were now friends. I'd go back and buy from him again.

The customer comes with expectations of a full measure of goods and services for the price he or she pays. When we exceed that measure, we have built a bridge of friendship for our friends, the customers, to come back again.

Thousands of years ago, a Chinese strategist wrote: "Use the normal to engage; the extraordinary to win." Normal service is commonplace. It's extraordinary service that gets attention.

Why do we drive past two or three grocery stores to shop at one farther away? Why do we always call a certain travel agent, or prefer to fly on a specific airline? Why do we buy one brand repeatedly, and ignore others?

The winning providers in every industry are not fighting for customers in the hope of winning. They have already won the battle by building bridges that take customers beyond their expectations.

We earn a preferential position for our product or service when the customer's experience consistently exceeds expectations. The key words are *consistently exceeds*. This level of expectation is a moving target. As satisfactory experiences accumulate, our threshold of standards for satisfaction increases. Customers learn their sophistication from their own experiences. Customers spread the word that makes great reputations, but only when the product or service is so good that the customer thinks it's worth talking about. A reputation is only what the customer thinks it is. The customer's perception is indeed the reality.

SHOW APPRECIATION BY DOING SOMETHING SPECIAL

The bridge of appreciation is constructed of special ways to say "thank you."

When Walt Herrick's customers go to their mailboxes in mid-November, they find a Thanksgiving card from Walt. He started this years ago before Thanksgiving cards were readily available. At that time, he sent his customers a handwritten, personal note.

I liked this idea so much that I stole it. Every year I send Thanksgiving cards to my customers. It's amazing how many people thank me for the cards at Thanksgiving and never mention the ones at Christmas. Obviously, the difference is in the number of cards they receive from friends and relatives. At Christmas, my card is one of dozens and gets lost in the clutter.

On Valentine's Day and during Secretaries' Week, I send candy or cookies to the secretaries of many of my customers. No competitor does, so the gift is seen as something special. It's amazing how many thank-you notes I receive. I'm amazed by the number of occasions when those secretaries do something special in return— like making sure I can get through to talk to their boss on the phone.

I remember Freddie Hoag in Portland, Oregon, who annually invited all of his customers to a "Customer Appreciation Night." He held a drawing for prizes such as dinner for two, tickets to a movie, or gift certificates. He decorated the store with balloons. He had gifts for the kids. He made it an event. Everyone went home with a small gift or prize and so did Freddie—"Customer Appreciation Night" was always his biggest sales day of the year.

Just saying "thank you" is important. Freddie always did that, but he also stood out from the crowd because he found an extra special way to show appreciation.

When we show appreciation to people, often they'll show appreciation back to us. When I sent flowers to a customer's house on their wedding anniversary his spouse called to ask if he knew "a Jerry Michaelson." He did— and called me to say "thanks."

When I sent a get-well card to a customer who was ill, his wife sent me a thank-you card.

When a bottle of champagne was delivered to the table where we were celebrating my son's graduation, I called to thank the sender (a supplier).

Thank-you Ideas

- Say "thank you," and offer a compliment
- Send a card or a handwritten note
  - ➤ on a holiday, other than Christmas
  - ➤ on a birthday
  - ➤ on a special occasion—for example, the anniversary of a purchase
  - ➤ a special event—for example, Secretaries' Week
  - ➤ after a purchase

- Send a gift when appropriate—for example, a wedding anniversary

- Write a note of praise; send it to the person's superior

NURTURE TRUST

A keystone is critical to the support of the structure. We shape the keystone of the bridge of trust by making promises we can keep.

Trust is an important ingredient of the structure of every bridge. Here are a few of the major ingredients of trust.

Be on time—every time. A certain company sends out a lot of seminar material each month that must be delivered on time. For a while, they used a carrier who always had an excuse when it didn't arrive on time. Now they use Federal Express because they found that their original slogan was true: "When it absolutely, positively has to be there overnight."

Whenever I meet with a customer, I make sure I arrive early so that I have a margin of safety. My rule is to arrive at least fifteen minutes before the meeting is scheduled to start. If it's a new location and I'm not sure of the routing, I plan to arrive even earlier.

Keep our promise. When we make a promise to a customer, keep the promise. Period.

Keep the customer informed. Keep the customer informed on all matters of interest in the relationship.

When a promise can't be kept, be sure to let the customer know as far in advance as possible. Not only is it courteous, it's good business.

Never, never should we be in the position of having the customer call us after the delivery date when we know that delivery will not be made on time. And, never tell the customer that something will be delivered at a specific time if we are not sure that we can keep the promise. When our credibility with the customer is lost, so is our business.

Tell the truth. I recall a sales trainee who, after observing several salespeople, told me that it was easy to build a customer's confidence: all we have to do is tell the truth. In matters of absolute fact, that's easy. In other instances that involve prediction of a future event, it's not quite so easy because we don't always know what the truth is. But we can state our views and expectations, and then keep the customer informed.

The Importance of Rapid Action in Building Trust

- **Delayed decisions** inevitably lose their positive quality. The longer it takes to get an answer, the more likely it is that the customer will be dissatisfied.

- **Slowness causes haste.** When a decision takes too long, it's execution requires rapid action, and may cause mistakes.

- **If we wait for approval from headquarters, we will be too late.** If the decision must be made through a bureaucracy, the customer will go elsewhere.

- **Rapid decision making produces rapid execution.** The shorter the decision time, the sooner we can communicate the decision and the more rapidly we can achieve service for the customer.

- **Rapid action is simultaneous action.** When swiftness and efficiency are at a maximum, all processes that could possibly be simultaneous are simultaneous.

VALUE THE CUSTOMER'S CULTURE

Customers want to cross bridges built to their cultural expectations.

At a restaurant in Germany, item 25 on the menu was a pan-fried perch fillet. Item 26 was a deep-fried perch fillet with tartar sauce. I asked the waitress if I could have item 25 with tartar sauce. "Nein, nein," was the reply. I knew that was no, but I didn't really understand why, because based on experience in my home country's culture I would have expected a "yes, certainly." In my travels I have come to expect rigidity in some cultures (where rules are rules).

It's important to respond to the customer's culture. In America we have a great variety of cultures. Customers have their own cultures with culture-specific expectations, and they bring their cultural expectations with them.

When I moved to Southern California, I was surprised to find that people never arrived anywhere on time and never offered an apology. A major contributor to that peculiarity could be the crowded freeways.

When I moved to New York City, I was surprised by what I first thought was an unfriendly attitude. I discovered it wasn't unfriendliness so much as the fact that many New Yorkers spend a great deal of time commuting, which involves adhering to rigid travel schedules. The lack of time for pleasantries was a casualty of the lifestyle.

A friend in Holland told me he encountered more culture shock when he moved from one part of Holland to another than when he moved halfway around the world to New Zealand.

When we cross a bridge to meet a customer, we often experience a clash of cultures. I've heard Europeans comment with disdain about the American waitress who arrives at the table saying, "Hi, my name is Judy, and I'm your waitress for the evening." Europeans generally expect a more formal relationship with a waiter or waitress.

I've seen the Japanese visitor bewildered because there is no agenda. The Japanese expect that for visitors every minute is scheduled—as it is in Japan.

Each customer brings his or her own culture along, wherever he or she goes. Our task is to build a bridge to the expectations of the customer's culture.

WHEN THINGS GO WRONG, MAKE THEM RIGHT

Build a bridge the customer wants to cross and make a friend—and win a new level of loyalty.

When things go wrong, we have a great opportunity to make a friend. Customers give us more credit for fixing problems promptly than they give us for months of operation with no errors.

Apologize. As a travel writer, I receive letters from travelers complaining about their experiences. One frequent complaint is: "They didn't even apologize." Be sure to apologize, and apologize profusely, then follow up with corrective action. The only mistake we can make in apologizing is not to apologize enough.

Leap into action. When the customer has a problem, what the customer wants is action—*now*. The more rapid the response, the more likely the customer is to be satisfied.

Studies by Abt Associates show that when the complaint takes too long to resolve, or involves too many people, customers become so dissatisfied with the process that they don't come back—even if the problem eventually is resolved satisfactorily.

Ask the customer's advice. Whenever a customer presents a problem, the best approach is simply to ask what adjustment he or she wants. I've usually found that whatever the customer wants is less costly than the offer I am prepared to make.

Refuse to argue. A friend describes his experiences with a certain airline this way: "When you have a problem, they show you the fine print and explain that if you hadn't flown on their airline, you wouldn't have had the problem." He refuses to fly on that airline anymore.

In contrast, I choose to fly mostly with a single airline that records my status as a frequent customer and makes me feel like they go out of their way to accommodate me. They have fixed mistakes they've made and they have also fixed mistakes I've made.

Make amends. In addition to apologizing, it's a good idea to find a way to atone for the customer's inconvenience. However, the atonement (or adjustment) must be one that makes the customer happy—otherwise we will lose the customer.

If the customer is happy with the atonement, the cost of the adjustment was a very good investment.

A fine hotel has a policy that when it can't fulfill a reservation, it offers the customer a free hotel room at another hotel, free transportation to and from that hotel, a free breakfast, and a free room on their next stay. This in atonement for an inconvenience is a good deal. Instead of getting mad, their customers say, "I'd like to have that problem at your hotel again."

When Things Go Wrong Take ALARM

A - Apologize

L - Leap (into action)

A - Ask advice (from the customer)

R - Refuse to argue

M - Make amends

BALANCE PRIORITIES

The bridges of champions are constructed by people focused on perfection in every component.

Everything we do, we must do well. There is no reason to be second-best anything. Winners know how to balance priorities.

Product *and* service. Both product and service must be outstanding in order to earn a reputation for being a great organization. Customers don't differentiate between the performance levels of the product or the service. For example, if we find the food in a restaurant to be very good and the service to be very bad, we are dissatisfied with the experience. The reverse is also true.

The customer *and* the associate (employee). Both are important. A senior executive at one large customer service organization said, "The associate must be considered first because we can't have happy customers unless we have happy associates." At another organization I heard, "The customer comes first, because without customers we don't need employees." Obviously, both are right—with a word of caution. When any associate thinks and acts like he or she is more important than the customer, problems arise. While associates may have to suffer situations where the importance of the customer becomes overwhelming, the customer will not long suffer the pompous or inattentive associate.

Selection *and* training. These are the most important elements necessary for having great people in any organization. The best organizations use the multiple interview technique: new hires are interviewed by the people with whom they will be working. Many organizations also have a professional psychologist assist in the initial screening. It's no surprise that at one of the top-rated hotels in the world, The Regent in Hong Kong, General Manager Thomas Axmacher showed me the most attractive and well-equipped training facilities I have seen in any hotel. The top organizations know how to select the best people and train them to be the best in their special field.

Keep up both the front of the house *and* the back of the house. In the hospitality industry, the front of the house describes the area the guest sees: the lobby, the restaurants, and the rooms. Everything else is the back of the house. When I toured the Hong Kong Regent's spotless inner corridors, General Manager Axmacher pointed to a ceiling that was being repaired, saying, "If we don't keep up the back of the house, our people will not notice things that need to be fixed in the front of the house." The reverse is also true. Customers who see shabby airplane interiors worry about the aircraft maintenance. A few local restaurants are so dirty on the outside that I never visit them.

BUILD BRIDGES TO EVERYONE

The purpose of a bridge is to serve the customer. Only those who build great bridges earn great customer loyalty.

Our customers are not just *anyone*; they are *everyone*.

Our customers are the people who receive our process, whether they are inside the company or outside the company. To avoid confusion, it's best to call internal customers *associates* and call those outside the organization *customers*. Some organizations use the term *stakeholder* to describe the various groups of customers—financial stakeholders, employee stakeholders, and so on.

There is only one standard: The customer is royalty. Everyone I know is my customer and everyone I know has the right to be treated like royalty.

Treating some people one way and some people another way does not work. Show me the person who treats someone like a customer and I'll show you a person who is capable of treating everyone like a customer.

A pattern of consistency underlies everything we do. The person who can be a friend, has friends. Getting and keeping customers is not something we can turn on and off like a light switch. People and organizations who have loyal customers have a sense of the customer in everything they do.

A sense of the customer is an art served by many sciences. We acquire knowledge of the science only through continual study of what the customer wants and how we can better serve that customer.

A customer is not a group. A customer is a very important individual—who may be a member of a group.

3

SUMMARY OF
GUIDING PRINCIPLES

GUIDING PRINCIPLES

Meet the enemy. Each of us is the architect and builder of the bridge of our own success or failure.

Know your customer. We build bridges to our customers by knowing where they are and what they want.

A regular customer is priceless. The best bridges encourage customers to make a lifetime of repeat purchases.

The customer is always right—simply because he or she is the customer.

Be the very best. The bridges to being the very best are constantly being reengineered and improved. We must run fast to stay good, and even faster to get ahead.

Have a written plan. The best plans build the best bridges, and the best plans are in writing—always.

Concentrate resources. Great bridges are built one at a time by people concentrated on the task.

Understand your processes. The first step in managing processes is to recognize the activities that comprise them. To learn more about processes, chart the flow of their activities.

Maintain high standards. Process standards (and measurements against these standards) provide the mechanism to ensure that we build a sturdy bridge to the customer.

Get benchmarking input. "It is right to learn, even from the enemy." —Ovid

Organize the power of teamwork. Build great bridges by strengthening the skills of individuals through the power of teams.

Improve and innovate. No bridge is ever as good as it can be.

Extend a warm welcome. The first step in getting the customer to cross the bridge is to offer a warm welcome—which is much more than just a friendly greeting.

Unleash the power of the customer's name. The customer's name is an important component of any bridge. Use it again, and again, and again.

Link the customer. Establish a bridge of links by introducing the customer by name to associates, and then strengthen those links by relating information about the customer.

Go to the limits of your authority. It is often better to beg forgiveness than to ask permission for an action. We can empower ourselves by assuming that we have all the authority we need except that which is expressly forbidden.

Make it easy to do business with your organization. Customers return to bridges they find easy to cross.

Listen, listen, listen and agree, agree, agree. Great bridge builders bite their tongues, keep quiet, and listen to what the customer has to say. Then they ask questions to get more information so they can solve the customer's problem.

Anticipate. Anticipate what customers want by looking at what they want from their own point of view.

Exceed expectations. Build a bridge of loyalty by giving more than a full measure.

Show appreciation by doing something special. The bridge of appreciation is constructed of special ways to say "thank you."

Nurture trust. A keystone is crutial to the support of the structure. We shape the keystone of the bridge of trust by making promises we can keep.

Value the customer's culture. Customers want to cross bridges built to their cultural expectations.

When things go wrong, make them right. Build a bridge the customer wants to cross and make a friend—and win a higher level of loyalty.

Balance priorities. The bridges of champions are constructed by people focused on perfection in every component.

Bridges to everyone. The purpose of a bridge is to serve the customer. Only those who build great bridges earn great customer loyalty.

4

THE ROLE OF MANAGEMENT:
LEADERS MUST LEAD

Regardless of who is at the helm when a ship runs aground, the captain is responsible. Similarly, the senior executive in every organization has the ultimate responsibility for building solid bridges of service performance.

The great hotels of the world are the premier theaters for experiencing outstanding service performance That is why comments from interviews with managers of fine hotels encapsulate the genesis of great service. As Mark Twain said, "All saints can do miracles, but few of them can keep a hotel."

LEADERSHIP

Senior management owns the implementation of systems, processes, and structure.

The greatest joy of my career was the first time we were rated the number one hotel by *Institutional Investors* magazine—also by *Conde Nast Traveler.* We held a staff party and gave out 1,350 custom-made watches. However, there is a lot of pressure when you are rated number one. You can expect negative press when you lose the top position and spend millions and never get it back.

Thomas Axmacher, General Manager
The Regent Hotel, Hong Kong

The leader must have a very clear vision of where the property should be in relation to the market. Then the basic objectives should be identified within that vision.

Nigel Roberts, General Manager
The Oriental Hotel, Singapore

Your vision should be something big. Something you reach for, go for, dream about, and keep alive. If you don't have a vision, you are retired. If you don't have your employees involved in that vision, you are not a leader, you are an old-fashioned manager. And when you have established what you want to do, determine what it takes to do it.

Horst Schulze, President and COO
Ritz-Carlton Hotel Company

The level at which the hotel can achieve full integration of new high technology equipment seems to be the key to success or survival in the future. However, we are aware that our service standards will not be measured by the technical utility of our systems, rather, the human touch that accompanies efficient service defines true standards, which eventually become traditions.

Kiyohito Minoshima, Senior Managing Director
Imperial Hotel Ltd., Tokyo, Japan

Managing a hotel is like managing a small town. You must be sensitive to the environmental and personal needs.

Thomas A. Klein, General Manager
Hayman Island, Great Barrier Reef, Australia

It is important to have key people in positions of responsibility. The staff must communicate with each other and develop a good working relationship. Resources must be focused on customer care and satisfaction.

William J. Kingston, General Manager
Westbury Hotel, Dublin, Ireland

We must create the idea that this property is a different environment and our staff must act differently when they are here. The back of the house must be equally clean and polished as the front of the house.

Thomas Axmacher, General Manager
The Regent Hotel, Hong Kong

Leadership is where the heart and soul come together with the processes.

Horst Schulze, President and COO
Ritz-Carlton Hotel Company

Our challenge is to create a committed team of leaders, who together have a strong passion to continually improve everything we do. Great organizations are on a never-ending journey of improvement.

Brian Hladnik, General Manager
Shangri-La Hotel, Singapore

SYSTEMS AND STRUCTURE

Strategies determine the organizational architecture necessary for successful implementation.

The most important ingredients in service quality are:

1st   Senior management has to be committed and understand the importance of total guest satisfaction.

2nd The right people with the right philosophy—this requires education.

Sandy Beall, Owner
The Inn at Blackberry Farms, Townsend, TN

One of the most important management concepts for our time is being ahead of our time. While it's important to know what the guest needs, it's also important to anticipate ahead of the guest's needs.

Joseph Kral, General Manager
Hyatt Aryaduta, Jakarta, Indonesia

It is important to create an environment where systems and structures are continually assessed against the needs of guests and staff. Continual simplification is the answer.

Brian Hladnik, General Manager
Shangri-La Hotel, Singapore

In order to have service quality, the physical plant must be in immaculate shape. The second requirement is more difficult—getting the staff where you want them to be.

Thomas Axmacher, General Manager
The Regent Hotel, Hong Kong

Information from guest comment cards, employee surveys, customer surveys, and reviews by an outside agency provide data to track performance and pinpoint areas for improvement.

James Haughney, General Manager
The Airport Hilton, Atlanta, Georgia

I have seen organizations that were very centralized where you could not express your own individuality. Regional approval was required to change the coffee shop menu. Decentralized organizations can adapt to the market. We have a few standards which we must follow; the rest are advisory guidelines.

Joseph Kral, General Manager
Hyatt Aryaduta, Jakarta, Indonesia

PEOPLE

People contribute most when they work in teams that focus on the customer.

Each person works with his team. The team reflects the spirit of hospitality.

> **Dario Regazzoni, Senior Vice President, Asia**
> **General Manager, Conrad, Hong Kong**

To serve is to empower yourself and others, and as a team create miracles.

> **Thomas A. Klein, General Manager**
> **Hayman Island, Great Barrier Reef, Australia**

Discretionary effort is usually the difference between a good hospitality experience and a bad one. It's important to create an environment in which people can contribute to the success of the business.

> **Clifford Ehrlich, Senior Vice President**
> **Marriott International**

The objective is retention of clients and that's due to people. When you build a hotel, they tell you it's locality, locality, locality. However, it's the people who work in the hotel who bring people back.

> **Bruce Banister, General Manager**
> **Brown's Hotel, London, England**

You cannot afford the risk of not having the right people. I place a serious amount of weight on my impression in the initial thirty seconds of the interview. You can tell a lot about someone's personality through their confidence, eye contact, and appearance. This is critical because the guest may only have a few seconds contact during which he or she judges our service.

> **Thomas A. Klein, General Manager**
> **Hayman Island, Great Barrier Reef, Australia**

By interviewing the best people in every category we have been able to create a profile of the kind of people we want to hire.

Horst Schulze, President and COO
Ritz-Carlton Hotel Company

Service is a profession.

Ted Kleisner, General Manager
Greenbrier Hotel, Greenbrier, NC

Whatever business you are in, you are in the service business because you serve customers. That service can only be accomplished through people.

Horst Schulze, President and COO
Ritz-Carlton Hotel Company

We put a lot of trust in our employees. Employees see it as enriching their jobs.

Anil Sampat, General Manager
Marriott Jeddah, Kingdom of Saudi Arabia

The customer should be able to identify with people, rather than the property. Then we've got to be able to deliver service and meet expectations. Here is where teamwork comes into play.

William J. Kingston, General Manager
Westbury Hotel, Dublin, Ireland

We are able to employ people like a former brain surgeon and a submarine navigator. As bright as these people may be, their bureaucratic background requires that they must be trained to take the initiative without worrying about being "covered."

Jaideep Mazumdar, General Manager
Grand Hotel Europe, St. Petersburg, Russia

I believe in the contribution of every employee toward the ultimate success of the hotel

Nigel Roberts, General Manager
The Oriental Hotel, Singapore

PROCESS MANAGEMENT

All work is a process. All processes can benefit from improvement and innovation.

We are a factory from metal to spoon. The client comes in the front door. When he leaves, you can see what you've achieved with what you've manufactured—the results of your work.

Felix M. Bieger, General Manager
The Peninsula, Hong Kong

Doing a lot of small things very well, will prevent bigger things from going wrong.

Nigel Roberts, General Manager
The Oriental Hotel, Singapore

If the cook has a problem and the stove isn't hot enough, we need to get him a hotter stove. I do not want to hear that we cannot produce quality because we have no budget. You cannot produce top quality if you do not have the proper tools. It is the manager's responsibility to provide his team with the best tools in order to do an excellent job.

Thomas Axmacher, General Manager
The Regent Hotel, Hong Kong

The day begins with a review of each department's log book. Here the managers write down the good and bad experiences—what went right and where and why guests complained. When a guest has a complaint, an apology is offered and in most cases the guests are seen personally by the general manager or his assistant where appropriate compensation is made.

Ronald F. Jones, O.B.E., General Manager
Claridge's, London, England

Good service is achieved by providing what the guest needs when and where it is needed.

Kiyohito Minoshima, Senior Managing Director
Imperial Hotels Ltd., Tokyo, Japan

Innovation and change are critical to success. Without these attributes, the best we can do is stand still.

Brian Hladnik, General Manager
Shangri-La Hotel, Singapore

Standards are established by heads of department working with their staff. However, the ultimate judge of the correctness and importance of the standards is the guest.

John Peariman, General Manager
Nutfield Priory, Redhill, England

Consistency is important. Anyone can produce a wonderful meal one day, it's important to do it every day.

> Jaideep Mazumdar, General Manager
> Grand Hotel Europe, St. Petersburg, Russia

CUSTOMER SATISFACTION AND ORGANIZATION PERFORMANCE

These are mutually supportive goals.

When managers are out with their people and with customers instead of sitting in their offices, productivity is higher and guest satisfaction is higher

> J. Willard "Bill" Marriott, Jr.,
> President and Chairman
> Marriott International

Our most important asset continues to be guest service. Our challenge is to make every aspect of internal and external performance work even better in order to maintain service integrity as our competition (and opportunity) becomes increasingly more global.

> Patricia Tam, General Manager
> Halekulani, Honolulu, Hawaii

No reason to say no to the customer. Our attitude is "The answer is yes, what's the question."

> Sandy Beall, Owner
> The Inn at Blackberry Farms, Townsend, TN

The caring attitude should come straight from the heart and be backed up by a happy expression. Good hotel management is the art from the heart.

Ronald F. Jones, O.B.E., General Manager
Claridge's, London, England

All I want is that the guest gets all the attention. We need to resolve problems and complaints before the guest leaves the hotel and we have to empower staff to do whatever it takes to make the guest happy—this requires extensive training.

Thomas Axmacher, General Manager
The Regent Hotel, Hong Kong

If you are full, you've still got to sell yourself and the best marketing is a referral from my guests to their friends.

Bruce Banister, General Manager
Brown's Hotel, London, England

I look at the arrival and departure list before I look at the figures, because if I don't have a guest in the house I don't need to look at the figures.

Felix M. Bieger, General Manager
The Peninsula, Hong Kong

When new employees come to orientation they are given a blank 3-by-5 card on which they are asked to state the goal of the hotel. The correct answer is guest satisfaction.

Joel Rothman, General Manger
San Diego Marriott Hotel and Marina

Our objective is to create outstanding memories for overnight guests and corporate America.

Sandy Beall, Owner
The Inn at Blackberry Farms, Townsend, TN

Our credo says that the genuine care and comfort of our guests is our highest mission—the most important thing we do.

Horst Schulze, President and COO
The Ritz Carlton Hotel Company

Senior Management has the Ultimate Responsibility for Providing the Leadership that Builds Great Bridges.

ABOUT THE AUTHOR

Gerald A. Michaelson is executive Vice President of the Asia/Pacific Division for Tennessee Associates International, where he assists organizations in achieving high levels of performance and customer satisfaction.

He has a broad base of experience at frontline and senior management levels in customer sevice, food services, lodging, retailing, and distribution services. He has served as national Vice President and member of the board of directors for the American Marketing Association.

Mr. Michaelson writes a regular column for Success magazine, and he is author of *Winning the Marketing War*, and *50 Ways to Close a Sale (and Keep Customers for Life)*. He is also an active member of the prestigious American Society of Travel Writers.

Gerald A. Michaelson, Executive Vice President, Tennessee Associates International, 223 Associates Boulevard, P.O. Box 710, Alcoa, TN 37701-0710, Phone: 800-426-4121, Fax: 423-982-1481

PRAISE FOR THE MANAGEMENT MASTER SERIES

"A rare information resource.... Each book is a gem; each set of six books a basic library.... Handy guides for success in the '90s and the new millennium."

Otis Wolkins
Vice President Quality Services/Marketing
Administration, GTE

"Productivity Press has provided a real service in its *Management Master Series*. These little books fill the huge gap between the 'bites' of oversimplified information found in most business magazines and the full-length books that no one has enough time to read. They have chosen very important topics in quality and found well-known authors who are willing to hold themselves within the 'one plane trip's worth' length limitation. Every serious manager should have a few of these in their reading backlog to help keep up with today's new management challenges."

C. Jackson Grayson, Jr.
Chairman, American Productivity & Quality Center

"The *Management Master Series* takes the Cliffs Notes approach to management ideas, with each monograph a tight 50 pages of remarkably meaty concepts that are defined, dissected, and contextualized for easy digestion."

Industry Week

"A concise overview of the critical success factors for today's leaders."

Quality Digest

"A wonderful collection of practical advice for managers."

Edgar R. Fiedler
Vice President and Economic Counsellor,
The Conference Board

"A great resource tool for business, government, and education."

Dr. Dennis J. Murray
President, Marist College

PRODUCTIVITY PRESS, Dept. BK, PO Box 13390, Portland, OR 97213-0390
Telephone: 1-800-394-6868   Fax: 1-800-394-6286

THE MANAGEMENT MASTER SERIES

The Management Master Series offers business managers leading-edge information on the best contemporary management practices. Written by respected authorities, each short "briefcase book" addresses a specific topic in a concise, to-the-point presentation, using both text and illustrations. These are ideal books for busy managers who want to get the whole message quickly.

Set 1. Great Management Ideas

Management Alert: Don't Reform—Transform!
Michael J. Kami
Transform your corporation: adapt faster, be more productive, perform better.

Vision, Mission, Total Quality: Leadership Tools for Turbulent Times
William F. Christopher
Build your vision and mission to achieve world class goals.

The Power of Strategic Partnering
Eberhard E. Scheuing
Take advantage of the strengths in your customer-supplier chain.

New Performance Measures
Brian H. Maskell
Measure service, quality, and flexibility with methods that address your customers' needs.

Motivating Superior Performance
Saul W. Gellerman
Use these key factors—non-monetary as well as monetary—to improve employee performance.

Doing and Rewarding: Inside a High-Performance Organization
Carl G. Thor
Design systems to reward superior performance and encourage productivity.

PRODUCTIVITY PRESS, Dept. BK, PO Box 13390, Portland, OR 97213-0390
Telephone: 1-800-394-6868   Fax: 1-800-394-6286

Set 2. Total Quality

The 16-Point Strategy for Productivity and Total Quality
William F. Christopher/Carl G. Thor
Essential points you need to know to improve the performance of your organization.

The TQM Paradigm: Key Ideas That Make It Work
Derm Barrett
Get a firm grasp of the world-changing ideas beyond the Total Quality movement.

Process Management: A Systems Approach to Total Quality
Eugene H. Melan
Learn how a business process orientation will clarify and streamline your organization's capabilities.

Practical Benchmarking for Mutual Improvement
Carl G. Thor
Discover a down-to-earth approach to benchmarking and building useful partnerships for quality.

Mistake-Proofing: Designing Errors Out
Richard B. Chase and Douglas M. Stewart
Learn how to eliminate errors and defects at the source with inexpensive *poka-yoke* devices and staff creativity.

Communicating, Training, and Developing for Quality Performance
Saul W. Gellerman
Gain quick expertise in communication and employee development basics.

Set 3. Customer Focus

Designing Products and Services That Customers Want
Robert King
Here are guidelines for designing customer-exciting products and services to meet the demands for continuous improvement and constant innovation to satisfy customers.

Creating Customers for Life
Eberhard E. Scheuing
Learn how to use quality function deployment to meet the demands for continuous improvement and constant innovation to satisfy customers.

Building Bridges to Customers
Gerald A. Michaelson
From the priceless value of a single customer to balancing priorities, Michaelson delivers a powerful guide for instituting a customer-based culture within any organization.

Delivering Customer Value: It's Everyone's Job
Karl Albrecht
This volume is dedicated to empowering people to deliver customer value and aligning a company's service systems.

Shared Expectations: Sustaining Customer Relationships
Wayne A. Little
How to create a process for sharing expectations and building lasting and profitable relationships with customers and suppliers that incorporates performance goals and measures.

Service Recovery: Fixing Broken Customers
Ron Zemke
Here are the guidelines for developing a customer-retaining service recovery system that can be a strategic asset in a company's total quality effort.

PRODUCTIVITY PRESS, Dept. BK, PO Box 13390, Portland, OR 97213-0390
Telephone: 1-800-394-6868   Fax: 1-800-394-6286

Set 4. Leadership (available November, 1995)

Leading the Way to Organization Renewal
Burt Nanus
How to build and steer a continually renewing and transforming organization by applying a vision to action strategy.

Checklist for Leaders
Gabriel Hevesi
Learn to focus day-to-day decisions and actions, leadership, communications, team building, planning, and efficiency.

Creating Leaders for Tomorrow
Karl Albrecht
How to mobilize all the intelligence of the organization to create value for customers.

Total Quality: A Framework for Leadership
D. Otis Wolkins
Consider the problems and opportunities in today's world of changing technology, global competition, and rising customer expectations in terms of the leadership role.

From Management to Leadership
Lawrence M. Miller
A visionary analysis of the qualities required of leaders in today's business: vision and values, enthusiasm for customers, teamwork, and problem-solving skills at all levels.

High Performance Leadership: Creating Value in a World of Change
Leonard R. Sayles
Examine the need for leadership involvement in work systems and operations technology to meet the increasing demands for short development cycles and technologically complex products and services.

PRODUCTIVITY PRESS, Dept. BK, PO Box 13390, Portland, OR 97213-0390
Telephone: 1-800-394-6868   Fax: 1-800-394-6286

ABOUT PRODUCTIVITY PRESS

Productivity Press exists to support the continuous improvement of American business and industry.

Since 1983, Productivity has published more than 100 books on the world's best manufacturing methods and management strategies. Many Productivity Press titles are direct source materials translated for the first time into English from industrial leaders around the world.

The impact of the Productivity publishing program on Western industry has been profound. Leading companies in virtually every industry sector use Productivity Press books for education and training. These books ride the cutting edge of today's business trends and include books on total quality management (TQM), corporate management, Just-In-Time manufacturing process improvements, total employee involvement (TEI), profit management, product design and development, total productive maintenance (TPM), and system dynamics.

To get a copy of the full-color catalog, call 800-394-6868 or fax 800-394-6286.

To view sample chapters and see the complete line of books, visit the Productivity Press online catalog on the Internet at *http://www.ppress.com/*

Productivity Press titles are distributed to the trade by National Book Network, 800-462-6420

TO ORDER: Write, phone, or fax Productivity Press, Dept. BK, P.O. Box 13390, Portland, OR 97213-0390, phone 800-394-6868, fax 800-394-6286. Send check or charge to your credit card (American Express, Visa, MasterCard accepted).

U.S. ORDERS: Add $5 shipping for first book, $2 each additional for UPS surface delivery. We offer attractive quantity discounts for bulk purchases of individual titles; call for more information.

ORDER BY E-MAIL: Order 24 hours a day from anywhere in the world. Use either address:
To order: *service@ppress.com*
To view online catalog on the Internet and/or to order:
   http://www.ppress.com/

INTERNATIONAL ORDERS: Write, phone, or fax for quote and indicate shipping method desired. For international callers, telephone number is 503-235-0600 and fax number is 503-235-0909. Prepayment in U.S. dollars must accompany your order (checks must be drawn on U.S. banks). When quote is returned with payment, your order will be shipped promptly by the method requested.

NOTE: Prices are in U.S. dollars and are subject to change without notice.

PRODUCTIVITY PRESS, Dept. BK, PO Box 13390, Portland, OR 97213-0390
Telephone: 1-800-394-6868   Fax: 1-800-394-6286